For Joan,
The best
librarian
a kid could ask for
- K.B.

For A.V.
- A.V.

Four Furious Flamingos

Copyright © 2022 Flying Pig Press

All rights reserved.

No part of this book may be reproduced or used in any manner without written permission except in the case of brief quotations embedded in book reviews.

Inquiries: kellybourne.ca/contact

ISBN: 978-1-7773896-2-8

First paperback edition: November 2022

FOUR
FURIOUS FLAMINGOS

written by Kelly Bourne
illustrated by Aparna Varma

Hey there!

Can you do me a favour?

My friends are having some
big feelings
and could use your help.

If you're not too busy,
would you mind telling them about a time
when you felt the same?

It would also help if you had any
ideas for how they might feel better.

Thanks a million.

1 ONE
LONELY LOBSTER

2 TWO EMBARRASSED EMUS

3 THREE CONFUSED CATERPILLARS

4 FOUR
FURIOUS FLAMINGOS

"are we next?"

5 FIVE NERVOUS NARWHALS

7 SEVEN SHY SHEEP

"Hi!"

8 EIGHT
DISAPPOINTED DUCKS

9	NINE
FRUSTRATED FIREFLIES

10 | TEN
TERRIFIED TARANTULAS

Here's some space to write them down, just in case you need to remember them the next time you're having big feelings.

Kelly Bourne
Author

When Kelly has big feelings, she likes to calm herself by taking a few deep breaths. She doesn't have a pet flamingo, but if she did, she would name it Francis. This is her second book.
You can learn more about Kelly at kellybourne.ca

Aparna Varma
Illustrator

Aparna grew up in the bustling city of New Delhi, India and often got in trouble for drawing all over her homework. Aparna studied Animation and Film in University and currently works in TV Animation Production in Toronto.
You can find more of her work at aparnavarma.com

Made in the USA
Las Vegas, NV
25 February 2024

86306657R00019